BUILDING AMERICA

THE CANALS

BUILDING AMERICA

THE CANALS

Raymond Bial

BENCHMARK BOOKS

MARSHALL CAVENDISH

NEW YORK

Benchmark Books
Marshall Cavendish
99 White Plains Road
Tarrytown, New York 10591-9001
Website: www.marshallcavendish.com

Book design by Clair Moritz-Magnesio
Map by Rodica Prato

Library of Congress Cataloging-in-Publication Data

Bial, Raymond.
    The canals / by Raymond Bial.
       p. cm. – (Building America)
    Includes bibliographical references and index.
    ISBN 0-7614-1336-7
    1. Canals—United States—Juvenile literature.   [1.Canals.] I. Title.
    II. Series:Bial, Raymond. Building America.
    HE395.A3B53 2001   386'.4'0973—dc21   00-065078

Photo research by Anne Burns Images
Cover by: Erie Canal Museum

The photographs in this book are used by permission and through the courtesy of: North Wind Pictures: title, 6, 8, 9, 10, 15, 17, 26, 50, back cover. Erie Canal Museum: 34, 36, 38, 40, 41, 42. Corbis: 12, 24. The Granger Collection: 14, 18, 20, 23, 28, 44, 48, 49. Middlesex Canal Association: 20.

Printed in Hong Kong
6 5 4 3 2

CONTENTS

Ships at the mouth of the James River prepare for loading. They will carry tobacco from the Virginia Colony across the Atlantic Ocean.

INTRODUCTION

The first Europeans in North America gazed upon the continent as a land of great promise. In the Old World, only the nobility could inherit wealth and privilege. However, in the "New World" any adventurous man was free to make his fortune. Yet how could these early explorers make their way through the dense, tangled forests that stretched from Canada to Florida?

The newcomers discovered that native peoples had already established a sprawling network for travel across North America—on land and by water. Indians journeyed on foot, softly padding in moccasins along paths through the forest. They used dogs, and later horses, to carry bundles or drag V-shaped sleds called travois (tra-VOY). Or they relied on water routes, especially in the eastern half of the continent. Native Americans paddled along rivers and across lakes in dugouts carved from logs and canoes made from birch or elm bark. When necessary, they portaged around rapids or to another stream. These early "river roads" stretched from the St. Lawrence River to the Great Lakes and through the Mississippi Valley all the way to the Gulf of Mexico.

Following the Indian trails, or traces, as they were often called, explorers, trappers, traders, and later settlers ventured on foot into the

Native Americans paddled canoes made of birch or elm bark along rivers and streams in the eastern woodlands of North America.

George Rogers Clark made his way down the Ohio River, then defeated the British at strategic forts along the Mississippi and Wabash Rivers.

wilderness. Or they relied on animals—horses, mules, and oxen—for travel and transportation. But it was often slow going, especially when wagons got stuck in the mud or deep snow. Like Native Americans, Europeans came to favor water routes. After sailing across the broad Atlantic in ships, British and Dutch colonists gathered along rivers. Among the most vital waterways on the eastern seaboard were the James River, which flowed through Virginia, and the Hudson River, which dominated New York.

Many other rivers and streams laced through the green forests—all leading into the heart of the wilderness.

Farther west, three long, wide rivers—the Ohio, the Mississippi, and the Missouri—and their tributaries, the Wabash, the Illinois, and hundreds of others, drained an enormous region from Pennsylvania to the Rocky Mountains. French explorers, known as *voyageurs*, used these rivers as trade routes. They paddled from Quebec on the St. Lawrence River in

Farmers living on the frontier shipped corn, pork, and other goods on flatboats that floated slowly down the Mississippi River.

eastern Canada, throughout the Great Lakes, and down the Mississippi River. To defend their newly claimed territory, the French built forts at key locations near present-day Detroit, Michigan, and in what became Indiana at Vincennes on the Wabash River and at Fort Wayne. They also established posts as far west and south as Fort de Chartres near present-day St. Louis and Fort Ascension, upriver from what is now Metropolis, Illinois.

Rivers shaped the early history and settlement of North America. Travelers glided along them in canoes to trade or do battle. In the French and Indian Wars, the British and the French battled fiercely for control of the North American interior along rivers.   Several years later, George Rogers Clark helped to defeat the British in the Revolutionary War in key battles on the Mississippi and Wabash Rivers. As the new United States expanded, homesteaders pushed westward, poling flatboats and keelboats along the rivers. They shipped corn, whiskey, pork, tobacco, and hardwood down these water routes. Small villages sprang up on the riverbanks, often around sawmills and gristmills, which used waterfalls and rapids as power for sawing timber and grinding grain. Tradespeople set up shop near the mills, and clusters of homes sprang up. In time, wharves, warehouses, and public buildings were built near these waters. Flowing generally east to west, the Ohio River was an especially important route. At one time, one fourth of all American people lived along this great river, which was described as a "poor man's highway."

French explorers Jacques Marquette and Louis Jolliet journeyed through the wilderness by canoe as far as the Mississippi River.

1

CANAL VISIONS

Many water routes—especially the Great Lakes and the Mississippi and Ohio Rivers—continue to be vital shipping routes to this day. Yet lakes and rivers were often not reliable. It was difficult to paddle or pole upstream. If a river was too shallow or narrow to carry boats, any hope of establishing a village on its banks was doomed. Rivers flooded seasonally and occasionally went dry during long droughts. Not all rivers joined, so goods had to be carried overland in portages to the next waterway. And often rivers simply did not run where people needed them. Canals were needed to link rivers, to open frontier lands for settlers, and to float goods to market.

The worth of canals in the New World was recognized as early as the 1600s by French explorers Jacques Marquette and Louis Jolliet. As they journeyed along the rivers and lakes of the upper Midwest, they came to what is now the location of Chicago. They concluded that this would be an excellent place to build a canal to link Lake Michigan with the Illinois River, which in turn flowed into the Mississippi. However, the first canals were not actually dug for more than a century, until the colonies had won their independence from England in the American

As a young man, George Washington worked as a surveyor, exploring the unsettled lands west of his home in Virginia.

The Appalachian Mountains stood as a barrier to settlers pushing into Kentucky and Ohio.

Revolution. Little more than ditches, these early canals were so narrow they could be crossed by a fallen tree. Poled or pulled by teams of mules, boats floated so slowly up and down the channels that a person on the towpath could easily stroll alongside them. However, in the days before steam engines powered paddleboats and trains, water remained the best way to transport people and goods.

George Washington is considered the father of the country—and of canal building in America. When he was a young man, he laid out tracts of land as a military surveyor. He then traveled widely while fighting in the French and Indian Wars. During these journeys, he became convinced of the great potential within the forests on the western edge of the young republic. When he became president, he considered waterways to be essential to the growth of the nation and proposed a canal to join the states on the Atlantic coast with the western wilderness.

However, canal building was hampered by the Appalachian Mountains, which stretch from Georgia to Maine. Individual ranges—the Smokies, Blue Ridge, Alleghenies, Adirondacks, Catskills, and Poconos—formed a long, high barrier of thickly wooded terrain. A few Indian trails through mountain passes had been discovered, notably the Cumberland Gap. But they rose up before their western slopes descended into Kentucky and Ohio. Settlers could pick their way through the passes, but how could canal beds carry water up these steep trails?

After the Revolutionary War, the rocky folds of the Appalachians hemmed in Americans along the Atlantic seaboard. Though the colonists had won their independence, the British still controlled much of the land to the north along the St. Lawrence River. France ruled the lands west of the Mississippi, known as Louisiana, and Spain held colonies in Florida and much of the Southwest. Washington knew that the three European powers at "the flanks and rear" of the United States could easily seize back much of the frontier. He observed, "The western states hang upon a pivot. The touch of a feather could turn them either way."

Yet the president envisioned the nation expanding westward. He lived in an era known as the Age of Enlightenment, in which people believed that extraordinary feats could be accomplished through art, science, and engineering. Even water could be made to flow upward, so boats could float over mountains. In 1783, Washington journeyed to some of his land along the Kanawha River in what is now West Virginia. This river flows into the Ohio River. Its headwaters are only thirty-five miles from the James River, which itself flows into the Atlantic Ocean. Washington reasoned that a canal linking the Kanawha and the James with the Ohio River would readily open up the fertile lands of the Ohio River valley—the future states of Ohio, Indiana, and Illinois—and the Great Lakes region.

Distracted by conflicts with Native Americans, Washington delayed his plan. When he next thought about canals, he decided that a better route might actually be the Potomac River. In 1785, after two terms as U.S. President, he became the head of the Patowmack Company, which undertook building a canal along the Potomac. After seven long years, a small canal—three quarters of a mile long—was eventually dug, so that boats could be paddled or sailed around a treacherous stretch of water known as Little Falls. But the canal had not reached over the mountains. Washington never realized his dream of surmounting the Allegheny range of the Appalachians. Early in its history, America simply lacked engineers and geologists, skilled laborers, and enough money to undertake such a massive effort as digging a canal. Yet Washington's vision had inspired others.

The canal along the Potomac River envisioned by George Washington was one of the first public ventures in canal building in the United States. Its towpath still winds along the Potomac River.

Horses patiently tow a barge loaded with goods along a canal through the countryside in the early 1800s.

2

LESSONS IN CANAL BUILDING

Robert Fulton, who was later credited with inventing the steamboat, predicted that canals would someday "pass through every vale, wind round each hill, and bind the whole nation together." He wisely turned to Europe for lessons on how to build canals. Among the engineering marvels he saw in England was a system of locks for raising and lowering water along a ninety-three mile stretch of canal that joined the Trent and Mersey Rivers. Until his death in

A river boat is loaded on Massachusett's Middlesex Canal. After ten long years of digging, the Middlesex became America's first successful canal.

1815, Fulton advocated a canal be built to join the Great Lakes with the Hudson River in New York. Eventually, the Erie Canal would do just that and become the greatest man-made waterway in North America.

After the American Revolution, over thirty canal enterprises had sprung up in the United States. By 1790, a number of short canals were dug. Some were no more than locks around shallows or waterfalls. Others were more ambitious. Like the short-lived Potomac Canal in Virginia, the Schuylkill and Susquehanna Canal in Pennsylvania sought the Ohio Valley as a destination. Begun in 1786 and completed in 1800, the twenty-two-mile Santee-Cooper Canal joined two rivers on the coastal plain of South Carolina. Designed by John Christian Senf, a Dutch immigrant and dug by African-American slaves, this was the first successful canal in North America. However, it was a private venture that benefitted only plantation owners.

In the late 1700s, with Yankee ingenuity and a skilled labor force, New England took the lead in public canals. Projects were undertaken on the Connecticut River and elsewhere. The first and most successful canal, the Middlesex Canal, ran from Boston Bay to the village of Middlesex on the Merrimack River. Chartered in 1793 and finished in 1803, this twenty-seven-mile canal was hailed as a great engineering feat. Undertaken by William Weston and Loammi Baldwin, the first American-born engineer, the canal had a high point at a millpond at the village of Billerica, Massachusetts. Usually, a canal's towpath ran along its bank, but the ingenious Weston devised a floating towpath made of wooden planks supported by pontoons that led straight over the pond. When they arrived at the millpond, the team of mules and the towboy simply continued over the planks while their boat floated over the water.

As with all early canals, men dug the Middlesex Canal entirely by hand, with pick and shovel. They hauled the soil away in dump carts devised by Baldwin and upon which the dump truck of today is based. When the earthen walls leaked, the soil had to be puddled, or mixed up. This process bound the soil particles more tightly and made the canal watertight. So the canal could cross ravines and rivers, men built large wooden troughs, known as aqueducts, set on stone piers. The canal actually flowed high over the Shawsheen and other streams.

The Middlesex canal also had to travel uphill in some places. So, locks had to be constructed with hydraulic, or watertight, cement. Known as trass, this cement was used to seal the joints between the stones. In Europe, along the Rhine River, builders used volcanic ash, but this material was too costly to ship across the Atlantic. Fortunately, Loammi Baldwin found a similar volcanic ash in the West Indies. Mistakes were made, notably the construction of a few wooden locks to save money. These locks eventually rotted and had to be replaced. However, Baldwin also invented a horse-powered pump to keep water out of the locks as they were built.

Accustomed to banging along rutted, bone-rattling roads in carriages and wagons, travelers on the Middlesex Canal marveled as they glided along the silver ribbon of water that coursed through the low hills, skirted a swamp, crossed the millpond, and then flowed through the aqueducts built high over the rivers. At the locks, they paused to refresh themselves at a tavern and soon were on their way again. American intellectuals, including the writer Henry David Thoreau, thoroughly enjoyed these experiences. The clergyman Edward Everett Hale claimed that "traveling on a canal is one of the most charming ways of travelling...to sit on the deck of a boat and see the country slide by you...is one of the exquisite luxuries."

figure . 1ere

This engraving exposes the workings of an eighteenth-century canal in France. A and C represent the gates of the lock, and D and E show the sluice gates for raising and lowering the water level inside.

Robert Fulton, an inventor and engineer, predicted that a network of canals would be constructed in the United States.

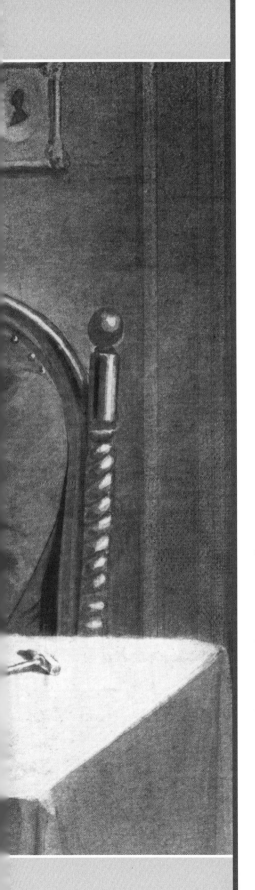

3

A NATIONAL PLAN

The Middlesex Canal proved that major canals could be built through the daunting landscape of America. Other people championed them, including Elkanah Watson. Having worked himself up from being an indentured servant to becoming an aide for Benjamin Franklin, Watson became fascinated by the canals of Holland and France. As he traveled with Franklin, who was then ambassador to France, Watson was especially impressed by the Canal du Midi. Unlike the lateral canals of Holland, Egypt, and China that flowed over level ground, this canal rose uphill, through locks, by bringing in water stored in reservoirs at higher levels. With V-shaped gates, this lock system was an engineering wonder based on designs made by Leonardo da Vinci during the Renaissance. The Canal du Midi was so well made that it still carries boats through the middle of France from the Atlantic Ocean to the Mediterrean Sea.

Years earlier, Robert Fulton had suggested a route through the northern part of the United States, linking the Hudson River with the Great Lakes. Elkanah Watson now agreed: "It appears that every natural advantage is in favor of New York." However, Watson had to wage a political battle before the first spadeful of dirt was turned. Although Thomas

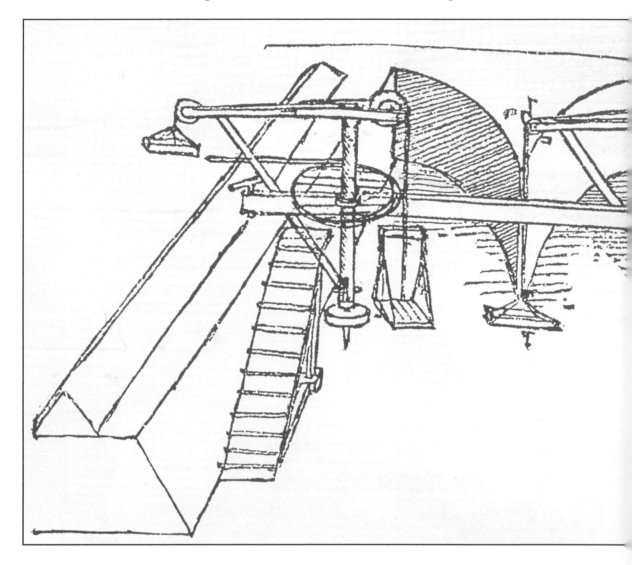

Jefferson, now president of the United States (1801-1809), also admired the French canals, he believed the states, not the federal government, should fund these enterprises—if they were even possible. About the New York canal, he declared, "It is a splendid project and may be executed a century hence." Although Jefferson's political opponents, the Federalists, were in favor of canals, they agreed that construction should not be funded by the federal government but by private industry. Finally, in 1803, Albert Gallatin, secretary of the treasury, conceived of a way to get canals built. In his 1808 *Report on Roads and Canals*, he suggested that the federal government become responsible for public works that were funded privately through joint stock companies. His report became a blueprint not only for canal building but for making other improvements throughout the nation.

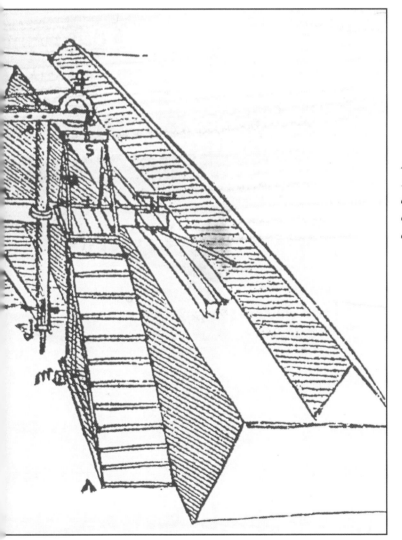

Among his many drawings, Leonardo da Vinci demonstrated a method for digging canals and building earthen embankments.

This painting by Frederick Edwin Church shows one of the most formidable obstacles to building the Erie Canal: the escarpment near Niagara Falls.

4

THE ERIE CANAL

The Grand Canal, as the Erie Canal was first known, was finally becoming a reality. Both Fulton and Watson may be credited for advocating the canal, but it was an energetic man named DeWitt Clinton, a state leader in New York, who initiated the project and drove the effort forward. When the digging began at Rome, New York, on July 4, 1817, no one knew how to overcome several obstacles—the hazards of the Mohawk River, with its sheer two-hundred-foot drop at Cohoes Falls, and the dizzying rise of the cliffs at Niagara. Yet the men bent to their work, singing with hearty confidence that they would find a way to complete the canal:

> *Then there's the State of New York, where some are very rich;*
> *Themselves and a few others are digging a mighty ditch,*
> *To render it more easy for us to find the way*
> *And sail upon the waters to Michiganiay—*
> *Yea, yea, to Michiganiay.*

The canawlers, as the workers came to be called, were paid at eighty cents a day. They threw themselves into the back-breaking task, axing a swath sixty-feet wide through the dense forest where surveyors had earlier staked out the canal bed. They chopped down ancient trees, some twenty feet around, and tore up the tangled roots. Once the brush and trees were cleared, they dug the canal bed with picks and shovels and cleared it with horse-drawn scrapers. They shattered rocks with a powerful new invention—blasting powder. They worked from dawn to dusk, fourteen hours a day during the summer, six days a week, always singing to ease the load:

> *We're digging a Ditch through the gravel,*
> *Through the gravel across the state, by heck!*
> *We're cutting the Ditch through the gravel*
> *So people and the freight can travel,*
> *Can travel across the state, by heck!*

The rowdy canawlers—Americans, and British, German, and Irish immigrants—were fed three huge meals a day, along with a tot of whiskey every two hours. As many as three thousand Irish "bogtrotters" worked on the big ditch. Men were released from militia duty, if they agreed to work on the canal. By 1819, these men had completed a ninety-six mile stretch between the towns of Syracuse and Utica.

How Locks Worked

These drawings (continued on pgs 30, 31)
show how a boat was lowered and raised
through a series of locks.

The mule driver and steersman carefully eased the barge into the lock.

When the barge was inside the lock, the crew swung the upper gates closed by pushing and pulling on the balance beam.

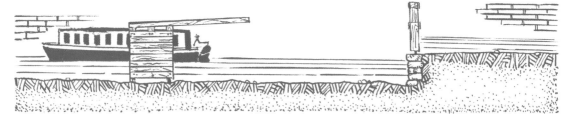

The lockkeeper opened up the wicket gates, and the water in the lock began flowing out into the lower part of the canal. As the water level in the lock fell, the boat was lowered until . . .

. . . it reached the lower level of the canal. Once the lower swing gates were opened, the packet could continue on its way. Another boat waiting to go in the opposite direction could then enter the lower part of the lock.

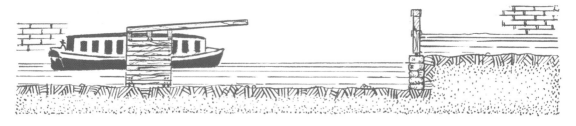

When the barge was inside the lock, the lower gates were closed . . .

. . . and the lockkeeper would open the filling ports to let in water from above, raising the water level in the lock and the barge to the upper level of the canal.

At very steep places along the canal a flight of several locks were needed. These flights of locks worked in the same way as the single lock.

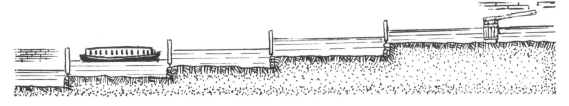

DeWitt Clinton celebrated the achievement of the Erie Canal by pouring water from the Great Lakes into New York Bay.

The workers faced one challenge after another. Among these were the Montezuma Marshes. Here, as soon as they dug the canal bed, the black mud oozed back into the channel. They finally had to build plank walls to hold back the muck. They were besieged by blood-sucking leeches and mosquitoes and had to watch for snakes and snapping turtles. Of these pests, the mosquitoes proved the greatest threat. These insects carried malaria, which left many of the men weak and feverish.

Yet the canawlers forged ahead, accomplishing the impossible. A stair of sixteen locks was engineered at the treacherous waters where the Mohawk and Hudson Rivers come together. An aqueduct had to be built around the falls at Cohoes and a new set of locks at Little Falls to replace those built in 1795. Each of the eighty-three locks on the Erie Canal was built of cut stone supported by timbers beneath of floor with two layers of wooden planks. Mitered gates that came tightly together at an angle were bound in iron and fitted with clever sluices and wickets to release water while the much larger gates remained closed. A single man could open and close the gates. Most ingenious, however, were the eighteen stone aqueducts over the rivers. Graceful and strong, they rested on piers joined by Romanesque arches.

Finally, in the fall of 1823, crews working from Lake Erie and Niagara met at Lockport, New York. In October 1825, to celebrate this great achievement, a boat called the *Seneca Chief* traveled the length of the Erie Canal. Amid grand speeches and festivities, Governor Clinton poured two kegs of Lake Erie water into the Atlantic Ocean to symbolize the joining of the waters by the canal. Boom times would soon come to New York State, which at last reached the fertile soils of the Great Lakes States.

A driver stands proudly with his team of three steady, hard-working mules along the towpath of the Erie Canal.

5

CANAL LIFE

The Erie Canal fostered a colorful new way of life. Towns sprang up along the towpaths; people even lived *on* the water. Their barges slowly plied up and down the ditch, under the guidance of a small crew: the captain, his wife (or other woman willing to cook and help as steersman), mule-tender, and hoggee, a boy who helped with the mules. The crew worked in six-hour shifts, every day, rain or shine. Teams of mules were also switched, at 7:00 A.M. and 1:00 P.M., and then at 7:00 P.M. and 1:00 A.M. The off-duty animals munched on hay

Mules were worked in six-hour shifts. One team of mules rested on the boat while the other towed the load down the canal.

and rested in a stable on the barge, which, due to the water's easterly flow, floated along about two miles an hour west and three miles an hour east.

Despite their reputation for being stubborn, mules were preferred as draft animals because they were less skittish than horses. Mules were often overworked and not always well treated. Some animals were marked with galls where they had been beaten, and many drowned in a tangle of harness when they slipped off the towpath and plunged into the canal. The mules were harnessed in tandem. A chain and a swinging wooden bar, known as a whiffletree, were attached to the harness behind the mules. A 250-foot towline connected the whiffletree to a post on the barge about a third of the way back from the bow on the starboard (right) side, the side near the bank. A pair of mules could pull a sixty-foot barge loaded with thirty tons of freight.

While the driver kept the mules trudging along the towpath, the steersman worked a tiller, a handle attached to the rudder, to head the boat straight down the canal. Mule drivers were tough characters who would "rather fight than eat." Endlessly walking the towpath, the hoggees had the hardest life on the canal, as expressed in this poem:

Hoggee on the towpath,
Five cents a day
Picking up the horseballs
To eat along the way!

Whole families lived in cabins on the barges, often called "line boats" because laundry was so often hung out to dry. Partitioned into a makeshift kitchen and "stateroom," the cabin was right next to the stable. Day and night, a cooking fire glowed in the stove, and people often lounged on deck in the shade of an awning. Small children occasionally fell overboard and drowned, prompting some mothers to tether their youngsters to the barge. The cabins were just big enough for two bunks about three feet wide, so children slept wherever they could find a place, often on the hay near the mules' feedbox.

At age five, children began to help out on the barge. As one man said, without children "The canal wouldn't run a day." Children grew up without attending school, knowing only the flow of the canal. The dream of most every boy was to get his own boat and become a captain by age sixteen. Girls hoped to marry a captain. Because life on the canal was so arduous, with few comforts and low pay, people could always find work on the boats.

The crew of the boat called the J. J. Belden *poses for a photograph. The crews on canal boats were often made up of family members.*

The Erie Canal continued to serve boat traffic for many years. Here, a boat passes through a barge lock around 1918.

Many people worked on the Erie Canal. Lock tenders, who had one or two helpers, were among the least-liked people. Appointed by politicians, they often weren't particularly honest. They allowed those captains who tipped them to move right through the locks, while others faced a long wait. Known to fight hard and drink heavily, they stole anything not "tacked down" on the barge. There were also inspectors, or towpath walkers, who watched for muskrat burrows in the earthen walls of the canal. If the canal leaked and water dropped too low, boats would become mudlarked, or stuck in the canal. But, of all those on the canals, the toll col-

Having made its way along the Erie Canal, this canal boat is being unloaded at the port in Buffalo, New York.

lectors were the most despised. Some bargemen attempted to slip past them in the black of night to avoid paying tolls, and everyone cheered when the canal was finally paid for and toll collection ended.

Despite the hardships of canal life, the length of the Erie Canal hummed with activity, which one man described as "the whole shebang of life." Along with barges, there were "bumboats," so called because they tied onto barges and hitched a free ride. Merchants sold household goods on the water, and craftsmen, such as tinkers and knife sharpeners, earned a living on bumboats, as did barbers, dentists, and the occasional entertainer. When he retired, one man so loved the canal that he placed a merry-go-round on a barge and charged for rides as he floated up and down its length.

Over the years, the Erie Canal was deepened, and by the Civil War, larger brightly colored passenger boats, known as packet boats, were put into service. Although line boats still carried both passengers and freights they were overshadowed by the packets, which carried droves of immigrants from the Atlantic ports to the Great Lakes. Harriet Martineau, a British journalist, suggested, "I would never advise ladies to travel by canal, unless the boats are quite new and clean." Similarly, Harriet Beecher Stowe, who wrote *Uncle Tom's Cabin*, commented, "Of all the ways of travelling, the canal boat is the most absolutely prosaic and inglorious." Philip Hone, the president of the Delaware and Hudson Canal Company, counseled against traveling on the Erie Canal at night, "The sleepers are packed away on narrow shelves, fastened to the sides of the boat, like dead pigs in a Cincinnati pork warehouse." By contrast, Charles Dickens, who disliked much of America, "heartily enjoyed" his canal trip, which he described as "gliding on at night, so noiselessly...no other sound than the liquid rippling of the water as the boat went on; all these were pure delights."

The impressive locks at the Upper Village of Lockport, New York, are shown in a lithograph from 1836.

6

CANAL CRAZE

With the success of the Erie Canal, America became canal crazy—from the Middlesex in Massachusetts' Berkshires to the Potomac in the soft hills of Maryland. Some canals were extended, and by the 1830s numerous feeder canals linked distant valleys to the main waterways. Many of these projects were unnecessary, leading to financial disaster, but no one wished to be left out in the great heyday of canals. Extended into Ohio and Illinois, canals linked the nation and brought boom times to the heartland by hauling its goods to market.

Sometimes, people simply went for "a coasting trip," as did this anony-
mous poet from Allen County, Indiana:

Once more on the deck I stand,
Of my own swift gliding craft—
The horses trot off on the land,
And the boat follows close abaft.
We shot through the turbid foam,
Like a bull frog in a squall—
And like the frogs, our home,
We'll find on the raging canawl.

This map illustrates the dense
network of canals that linked our
country before rails and roads
took their place.

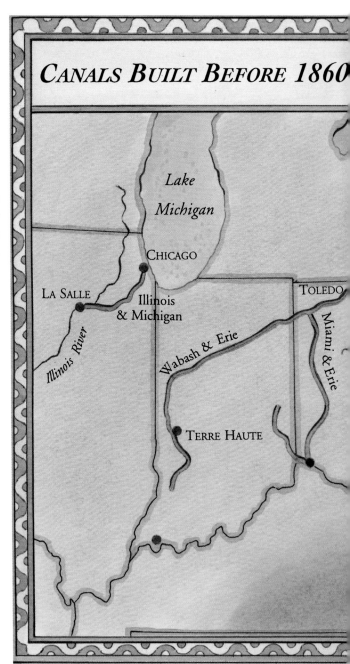

CANALS BUILT BEFORE 1860

Lake Michigan

CHICAGO

LA SALLE

Illinois & Michigan

Illinois River

TOLEDO

Wabash & Erie

Miami & Erie

TERRE HAUTE

In the 1830s, the country was bustling with industry and trade. Many people eagerly left the farm and went to work for a wage, often sliding into debt, so they could purchase goods shipped between the thriving cities of the East and the West. In broadsides and newspapers ads, boosters promoted their new towns as wonderful places. Eastern investors were

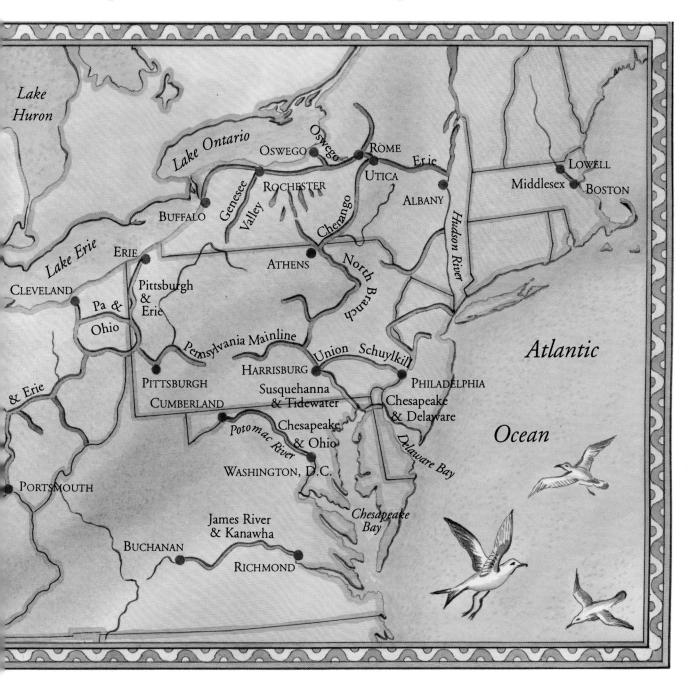

keenly interested in cashing in on the wealth to the west of the Appalachian Mountains. Both the Erie Canal and the National Road—the first major western route into the heartland—had been completed, and steamboats plied the Ohio and Mississippi Rivers in what became a golden age that continued to mid-century.

An observer, Robert H. Wiebe, wrote about what he called "a vibrant public process: marching, chanting, disputing, debating, voting." A person simply had to "get into it. Ask nobody's permission, defer to nobody's prior claim. Just do it." In an energetic movement goods and people floated by canal and river from the Eastern cities all the way to New Orleans. In the 1840s, however, railroads began to lay tracks along river valleys and canal routes. By mid-century, much of the nation's transportation had become a mixture of turnpikes, canals, and railroads that joined the branches of the major rivers. The daily rhythm of the river was marked by the bells and the whistles of the steamboats that linked the towns along the banks.

Entitled "A Night on the Hudson," this Currier & Ives lithograph from 1864 depicts boats continuing their journey down the Hudson River from the Erie Canal.

An elegant steamboat stops on the bank of the Mississippi River to collect fuel in this Currier & Ives lithograph called "Wooding Up."

Here is a popular folk song from the "steamboatin' days" on the Ohio and Mississippi Rivers.

> *You see that boat a-comin'*
> *She's comin' roun' the ben'*
> *And when she gets in*
> *She'll be loaded down again.*

By 1870, railroad tracks, like rows of stitches, crisscrossed the country, bringing an end to the elaborate system of canals that connected the rivers and streams. In the days of Mark Twain, flatboats, rafts, and skiffs that plied the rivers and streams were replaced by the huge barges and steamboats that chugged up and down the Mississippi, Ohio, and

Passengers gaze upon a quiet village as their steamboat ties up for a brief pause. Soon they will continue gliding along the Mississippi River.

Missouri Rivers. Yet these steamboats too quickly went the way of the canals, as Americans came to rely on the rails.

Today, huge barges still move up and down the great rivers, but they now serve only as links to railroads. Stretches of the Erie Canal remain in use; others, such as the Chesapeake and Ohio Canal in Maryland and short sections of canals in Ohio and Indiana, have been preserved as historical sites, parks, and trails for hikers and bicyclists. Most canals have been long abandoned, however. Reclaimed by fields and forests, the stonework of aqueducts and locks haunt the landscape as reminders of a time gone by.

GLOSSARY

aqueduct a bridge-like structure that carries a waterway over a low area, such as a valley

barge a flat boat for transporting freight and other goods

berm an earthen wall, sometimes forming the side of a canal

canal a man-made waterway for transporting people and cargo

canal boat a freight boat for use on a canal, having a small cabin for the captain and his family

hoggee a boy who helped a mule-tender

lock a short section of a canal with gates at each end. The level of water in the lock is raised or lowered to convey a boat to the next level of the canal

packet a passenger boat that also carried goods and mail on a regular schedule

puddling a process by which soil particles are mixed and bound more tightly, used to make the canals watertight

towline a rope used to pull a canal boat

towpath a path on one side of a canal along which horses or mules pulled a boat

trass waterproof cement used to seal the joints between the stones in a canal lock

whiffletree a swinging wooden piece attached to the mules' harness and a towline

FURTHER INFORMATION

BOOKS FOR YOUNG READERS

Boyer, Edward. *River and Canal*. New York: Holiday House, 1986.

Cooper, Jason. *Canals*. Vero Beach, FL: Rourke Enterprises, 1991.

The Erie Canal. Peterborough, NH: Cobblestone Publishers, 1982.

Hill, Lee Sullivan. *Canals are Water Roads*. Minneapolis: Carolrhoda Books, 1997.

McNeese, Tim. *America's Early Canals*. New York: Crestwood House, 1993.

Oxlade, Chris. *Canals and Waterways*. New York: F. Watts, 1994.

Rickard, Graham. *Canals*. New York: Bookwright Press, 1988.

Spangenburg, Ray. *The Story of America's Canals*. New York: Facts on File, 1992.

Tames, Richard. *History of Canals*. Hove, England: Wayland Publishers, 1996.

WEBSITES

American Canal Society
http://www.canals.com/ACS/acs.html

Canal Society of Indiana
http://www.indcanal.org/

The Canal Society of Ohio
http://my.ohio.voyager.net/~lstevens/canal/csoo/

Chesapeake & Ohio Canal
http://www.nps.gov/choh/

Erie Canal Museum
http://www.eriecanalmuseum.org/

Erie Canal Online
http://www.syracuse.com/features/eriecanal/

National Canal Museum
http://www.canals.org/

New York State Canal System
http://www.canals.state.ny.us/

North American Canals
http://www.canals.com/northam.htm

Ohio & Erie Canal
http://www.ohio-eriecanal.com/

Old Metamora, 1838 Canal Town
http://www.metamora.com/

BIBLIOGRAPHY

American Waterways: Canal Days. Carlisle, MA: Discovery Enterprises, 1997.

Andrist, Ralph K. *The Erie Canal*. New York: American Heritage, 1964.

The Best from American Canals. York, PA.: American Canal and Transportation Center, 1980.

Bigham, Darrel E. *Towns & Villages of the Lower Ohio*. Lexington, KY: University Press of Kentucky, 1998.

Bourne, Russell. *Floating West: The Erie and Other American Canals*. New York: W. W. Norton, 1992.

Brownstone, Douglass L. *A Field Guide to America's History*. New York: Facts on File, 1984.

Condon, George E. *Stars in the Water: the Story of the Erie Canal*. Garden City, NY: Doubleday, 1974.

Fatout, Paul. *Indiana Canals*. West Lafayette, IN: Purdue University Press, 1972.

Hahn, Thomas F. and Emory L. Kemp. *Canal Terminology of the United States*. Morgantown, WV: Institute for the History of Technology & Industrial Archaeology, 1999.

Hawke, David Freeman. *Everyday Life in Early America*. New York: Harper & Row, 1988.

Ridge, Martin. *Atlas of American Frontiers*. Chicago: Rand McNally, 1993.

Shank, William H. *Towpaths to Tugboats: a History of American Canal Engineering*. York, PA.: American Canal and Transportation Center, 1992, 1982.

Shaw, Ronald E. *Canals for a Nation: the Canal Era in the United States, 1790--1860*. Lexington, KY.: University Press of Kentucky, 1990.

Tunis, Edwin. *Colonial Living*. New York: Crowell, 1976.

Tunis, Edwin. *Frontier Living*. New York: Crowell, 1976.

Tunis, Edwin. *The Young United States, 1783-1830: A Time of Change and Growth, A Time of Learning Democracy, A Time of New Ways of Living, Thinking, and Doing*. New York, World Publishing Co., 1969.

INDEX

Page numbers in **boldface** are illustrations

Raymond Bial has published over fifty critically acclaimed books of non-fiction and fiction for children and adults. His photo essays for children include *Corn Belt Harvest, County Fair, Amish Home, Cajun Home, Frontier Home, Shaker Home, The Underground Railroad, Portrait of a Farm Family, With Needle and Thread: A Book About Quilts, Mist Over the Mountains: Appalachia and Its People, The Strength of These Arms: Life in the Slave Quarters, Where Lincoln Walked, One-Room School, A Handful of Dirt,* and *Ghost Towns of the American West.*

He has written Lifeways, a series published by Marshall Cavendish about Native Americans, traveling to tribal cultural centers, to photograph people, places, and objects that reflect the rich history and social life of Indian peoples.

Building America is the author's second series with Marshall Cavendish. As with his other work, Bial's love of social and cultural history and his deep feeling for his subjects is evident in both the text and the illustrations.

A full-time librarian at a small college in Champaign, Illinois, he lives with his wife and three children in nearby Urbana.